Kate DiCamillo

My Favorite Writer

Lucy Briggs

WEIGL PUBLISHERS INC.

Published by Weigl Publishers Inc.
350 5th Avenue, Suite 3304, PMB 6G
New York, NY 10118-0069
USA
Web site: www.weigl.com

Library of Congress Cataloging-in-Publication Data

Briggs, Lucy.
   Kate DiCamillo / by Lucy Briggs.
      p. cm. -- (My favorite writer)
   Includes index.
   ISBN 1-59036-283-7 (alk. paper) -- ISBN 1-59036-289-6 (soft cover : alk. paper)
   1. DiCamillo, Kate--Juvenile literature. 2. Authors, American--21st century--Biography--Juvenile literature. 3. Creative writing--Juvenile literature. I. Title. II. Series.
   PS3604.I23Z59 2005
   813'.6--dc22

2004029925

Project Coordinator
Tina Schwartzenberger

Substantive Editor
Frances Purslow

Design
Terry Paulhus

Layout
Jeff Brown
Kathryn Livingstone

Photo Researcher
Kim Winiski

Printed in the United States of America
1 2 3 4 5 6 7 8 9 0 09 08 07 06 05

Contents

Kate DiCamillo

MILESTONES

1964 Born on March 25 in Philadelphia, Pennsylvania

1969 Moves to Clermont, Florida

1987 Receives an English degree from the University of Florida

1994 Moves to Minneapolis, Minnesota

2000 *Because of Winn-Dixie* is published

2001 *Because of Winn-Dixie* is named a Newbery Honor Book

2001 *The Tiger Rising* is published

2001 *The Tiger Rising* becomes a National Book Award finalist

2003 *The Tale of Despereaux* is published

2004 *The Tale of Despereaux* wins the Newbery Medal

2005 The movie, *Because of Winn-Dixie*, is released

Do you remember Rumplestiltskin? He was the little man in the fairy tale who spun straw into gold. Kate DiCamillo is also a spinner. However, Kate does not spin straw. She takes ordinary ideas and spins them into stories.

Readers often wonder how writers learn the magic that changes ordinary words into spellbinding stories. Kate has an eye for detail and an ear for words.

When Kate grew up, she worked in the children's section of a book warehouse. There, she remembered the wonders of children's literature. She decided to write for children.

Kate loves telling stories. She creates prize-winning stories containing characters that readers remember. Spunky India Opal Buloni in *Because of Winn-Dixie* has a smiling and talented dog. The caged and **majestic** tiger in *The Tiger Rising* helps lonely Rob Horton find courage and friends. The big-eared mouse, Despereaux Tilling, is magical. Kate's books are popular with children, earning her lasting positions on bestseller lists.

Early Childhood

Kate DiCamillo was born on March 25, 1964, in Philadelphia, Pennsylvania. During her early years, she suffered from **recurring** pneumonia. Pneumonia is an illness that affects the lungs. Kate's illness helped develop her great imagination. When she was too ill to play with friends, Kate turned to books for company. She developed a love for books. She played dress up with her dog, Nanette, a black standard poodle. Kate often dressed Nanette in a green ballet tutu. When Kate grew a little older, she dressed Nanette as a disco dancer.

When Kate was 5 years old, her family moved to Florida. Kate's doctor hoped the warm weather would be good for her lungs. Kate's father separated from the family. Kate, her mother, and her older brother, Curt, settled in the small town of Clermont, Florida.

> "The town was small, and everybody knew everybody else.... It was all so different from what I had known before, and I fell swiftly and madly in love."
> **Kate DiCamillo**

■ Kate's hometown of Philadelphia, Pennsylvania, is known as the "Birthplace of the Nation." Both the Declaration of Independence and the Constitution were drafted in the city.

Clermont is in central Florida. It is in an area with many lakes, fruit orchards, big trees, and warm weather. Kate loved Clermont. She liked knowing many people in the small town. She enjoyed climbing the trees, and she had fun swimming in the lakes. Most of all, though, Kate enjoyed reading.

Kate read many books. The books she read as a child helped her learn to write well. Reading helped Kate develop a love of stories.

Writers often include people, places, or events from their own lives in their stories. Kate's experiences in Clermont often appear in her books. For example, when Kate first moved to Florida, she noticed that people spoke differently than she was used to hearing. People spoke slowly. They used words such as "y'all" and "ma'am." These details appear in Kate's first book, *Because of Winn-Dixie*.

■ This late 1950s postcard shows Clermont's orange groves. Today, Clermont is known for its Christmas-tree farms.

Growing Up

Every day during the summer, Kate's mother took her to the library.

Kate enjoyed swimming in the lakes surrounding Clermont. This 1950s postcard shows Jaycee Beach on Lake Minneola in Clermont.

Kate does not talk much about her childhood. Her fans do not know a great deal about Kate's experiences growing up. She rarely mentions school. Still, Kate understands children. She says that "any child on a school bus knows that the world is **complicated** and rough." Kate used this knowledge in *The Tiger Rising*. In the story, Rob faces daily **torment** from bullies.

Kate says she knows that children have worries, too. She writes about some of these worries. Moving to a new place, seeking new friends, losing a parent, and having a pet are ideas explored in her books.

Since Kate loved to read, it is no surprise that she visited the library often. Clermont's library was located in an old house. Every day during the summer, Kate's mother took Kate and Curt to the library. At home, their mother read to them often.

Kate says that when she was ill, she learned to rely on stories as a way of understanding the world. "A lot of times a book can shed light on what's going on in your life," she says. "It can also be a brief escape."

After graduating from high school, Kate attended Rollins College, the University of Central Florida, and the University of Florida at Gainesville. She has a Bachelor of Arts degree in English from the University of Florida. While working toward her degree, Kate read many books. She did not train to be a writer, but her professors thought that she wrote well. Kate decided she would be a writer.

For the next 9 years, Kate called herself a writer, but she did not write. She says that she lived the writer lifestyle, even though she did not write. "I spent my twenties wearing black turtlenecks and looking thoughtful and intense," she admits.

Inspired to Write

Kate DiCamillo's professors at university told her that she had "a way with words." Another instructor praised the details in an essay she had written. These comments inspired Kate. She decided to be a writer. For 14 years, she read about writing. Finally, she began to write.

Kate studied English in Turlington Hall at the University of Florida. A 30-million-year-old rock sits in front of the building.

Working at Walt Disney World, Kate observed many children. This helped her when she began to write books for children.

Like many artists, writers, and musicians, Kate worked several jobs to pay the bills. She avoided office work. One of Kate's earliest jobs was at a fast-food restaurant. She remembers receiving a 5-cent raise as a reward for good work. Kate also had other kinds of jobs. She planted flowers in a greenhouse. She sold tickets at Circus World. She worked on the rides at Walt Disney World. She also called bingo numbers at a children's camp. Although these were not writing jobs, they helped Kate. These jobs allowed Kate to observe parents and children— many children.

When Kate was almost 30 years old, she moved to Minneapolis, Minnesota. There, she found a job that changed her life. She worked on the children's floor of a book warehouse. She selected books to send to bookstores. Kate began to read the children's books. She was amazed at how interesting and well written they were.

When Kate began writing, she wrote short stories. She rewrote her stories many times, but none of them were published.

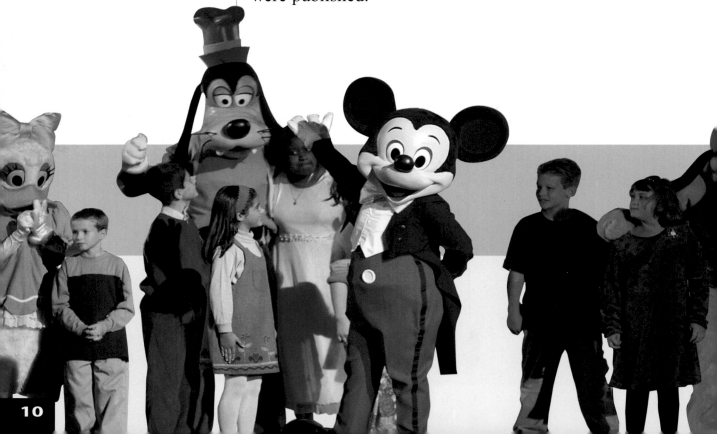

The winters in Minnesota are cold and long. Kate longed for the warm weather in Florida. She lived in an apartment that did not allow pets, and Kate missed her dog. She also longed to see her friends and hear their slow southern speech.

The cold and loneliness inspired Kate to write *Because of Winn-Dixie*. Kate claims that one day she heard a soft, southern voice in her head. The voice said, "I have a dog named Winn-Dixie." Kate used this sentence to begin her first children's novel.

In 1994, Kate moved to Minneapolis. Winter temperatures in the city average 5° Fahrenheit (15° Celsius).

Favorite Authors

Kate loved to read. Her favorite books include *Twenty-One Balloons* by William Pene du Bois, *The Secret Garden* by Frances Hodgson Burnett, *The Yearling* by Marjorie Kinnan Rawlings, and *Somebody Else's Shoes* by C. J. Wilson. Another one of her favorite children's books is *Holes* by Louis Sachar. One book that Kate read while working in the book warehouse impressed her so much that she decided to become a children's writer. The book is *The Watsons Go To Birmingham, 1963* by Christopher Paul Curtis.

Learning the Craft

Kate says people should not try to write unless they read.

Kate began writing by reading. She expanded her love and knowledge of reading by earning an English degree. Kate believes that reading has greatly helped her writing. Kate says people should not try to write unless they read. She reads certain books many times to inspire herself about the art of writing. One book is *Art and Fear.* Kate says this book "always gives me the strength to go on."

Although her life goal was to be a writer, Kate did not begin writing until she was almost 30 years old. She started writing short stories. Kate made sure that she wrote 2 pages a day, 5 days a week. When she worked at the book warehouse, she woke up at four o'clock in the morning to write two pages before leaving for her job. Rewriting is also important to Kate. She writes a first **draft** of each story. Two weeks later, she writes a second draft.

In *The Tiger Rising*, Rob Horton enjoys carving little sculptures out of wood. He decides to make a tiger, but when he looks down, he has **whittled** a girl. His hands took over. Kate claims that the same thing happens with her writing.

Kate used what she called an "exercise philosophy" to her writing: two pages a day, every day. The idea came from Kate's running schedule.

One day, a little girl with a southern drawl popped into Kate's head. *Because of Winn-Dixie* followed. Kate says that she has to "let her characters tell their own stories." She does not create her characters or her stories. Instead, the characters come to her. They tell Kate their stories. Then, she writes the stories down on paper.

Kate writes about what she knows. Her early stories are set in Florida, where she was raised. Kate grew up in a single-parent home. Her stories have characters who long for an absent parent. India Opal, Rob, Sistine, the Princess, and Miggery Sow share this bond of loneliness.

Although Kate claims she is still unsure of her talent, her books show that she is an experienced writer. Kate says that writing is more about hard work than talent. She never wants to write, but she is always glad when she has written. It takes Kate about 1 year to complete a novel.

■ Florida's Everglades National Park is home to pine trees and palmettos. These trees often appear in Kate's stories.

Getting Published

Publishing companies reject many pieces of writing. Kate DiCamillo estimates that she has received as many as 500 rejection letters. Still, she did not give up.

For many years, Kate planned to write. She dreamed about writing. Finally, Kate began writing. She sent a short story to a magazine. The editor turned it down. For 6 years, Kate wrote short stories that publishers rejected. Then, she changed her approach.

Kate wrote the children's novel, *Because of Winn-Dixie*. She worked full-time even though she had received a **grant** from the McKnight Foundation to write a book. She wrote every morning. After about a year, the book was complete.

> "I wrote a short story. It was a very bad short story. I rewrote it. It got **marginally** better. I rewrote it again. And again. And again. I sent it off to a magazine. They rejected it."
> Kate DiCamillo

The Publishing Process

Publishing companies receive hundreds of **manuscripts** from authors each year. Only a few manuscripts become books. Publishers must be sure that a manuscript will sell many copies. As a result, publishers reject most of the manuscripts they receive.

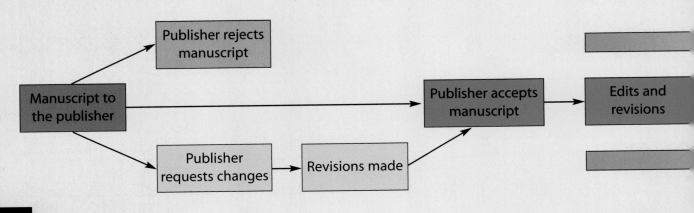

Candlewick Press published *Because of Winn-Dixie* in 2000. It became a bestseller. *The Tiger Rising* was published in 2001. In 2003, *The Tale of Despereaux* followed. All of Kate's books have won awards. Kate says that she was "stunned and very, very happy" when her first novel, *Because of Winn-Dixie*, won an award.

Kate promises not to stop writing. Her next book is called *The Miraculous Journey of Edward Tulane.* She continues to polish her collection of short stories. Kate has some very good advice for writers who hope to be published. "Keep writing. Keep submitting. The race goes not to the brilliant but to the disciplined, to those who **persevere**."

Inspired to Write

The need for warmth and the desire for a pet inspired Kate to write during her first winter in Minneapolis. She could not afford to travel to Florida. Instead, she used her memory and her imagination to recreate the world for which she longed.

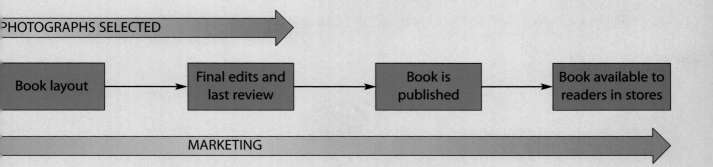

Once a manuscript has been accepted, it goes through many stages before it is published. Often, authors change their work to follow an editor's suggestions. Once the book is published, some authors receive royalties. This is money based on book sales.

PHOTOGRAPHS SELECTED →

| Book layout | → | Final edits and last review | → | Book is published | → | Book available to readers in stores |

MARKETING →

Writer Today

Kate DiCamillo still lives in Minneapolis, Minnesota. She no longer **pines** for a small town in Florida. Kate enjoys the cold winters, spending time with her new friends, and the **cultural** life in Minneapolis.

Kate no longer works at the book warehouse. She is much too busy. She receives many letters from young fans and tries to answer them all. Kate is booked for visits to schools and children's fairs more than 1 year in advance.

In 2002, Kate accepted the Dorothy Canfield Fisher Award at Vermont Technical College. Children in grades 4 to 8 in Vermont schools read books on a list and vote for their favorite. *Because of Winn-Dixie* was a clear winner. After accepting the award, Kate answered questions and posed for pictures. She enjoys visiting with her young fans.

Kate is not married. Although she has no children of her own, Kate spends time with her brother, Curt's children—Luke, Roxanne, and Max. Kate does not have a dog. She spends too much time traveling to be able to care for a pet.

■ Kate is modest about her success. She says, "All I have is the desire and discipline to take the first draft to the fifth draft."

Kate continues to read many books. Her favorite books are novels, as she loves a good story. Kate also enjoys visiting toy stores. She says, "It's the kid in me that creates. You have to honor that something inside that's whole and unbroken."

Despite her success, Kate sometimes feels unsure and fearful about her ability to write. For the past 5 years, she has been a member of a writers' **critique** group. The group members read each other's work and offer suggestions and support.

Kate is working on a number of writing projects. She hopes to publish a collection of short stories soon.

Kate spent time on the *Because of Winn-Dixie* movie set. She even played with the smiling dog that acted as Winn-Dixie.

Popular Books

Kate DiCamillo's children's books are very popular. Young readers find her characters realistic. Her books have won many awards. Kate is a new writer who has not published many books.

AWARDS
Because of Winn-Dixie

2001 Newbery Honor Book

2001 Josette Frank Award

2002 Dorothy Canfield Fisher Children's Book Award

2002 Maine Student Book Award

2002 Massachusetts Children's Book Award

2002 Charlotte Award

2002-2003 Hoosier Award

2003 Young Reader's Choice Award

Because of Winn-Dixie

Because of Winn-Dixie is Kate's first published book. She wrote this story during a terrible winter in Minnesota. Everything that Kate was homesick for—her friends, her dog, and the warm weather of her Florida home—is talked about in this book.

Because of Winn-Dixie celebrates dogs and friends. It takes place in a small town in Florida. The main character is a spunky, young girl named India Opal Buloni. India Opal moves to a new town and needs to make new friends. Her first friend is an ugly stray dog with a big smile. She names him "Winn-Dixie" after the supermarket in which she found him.

Winn-Dixie is a very special dog. He senses when people are lonely and brings them together. Soon, India Opal has a circle of new friends.

Because of **Winn-Dixie**

There never was a town in greater need of a change, or a dog in greater need of a town.

KATE DiCAMILLO

The Award-Winning Bestseller
Now a Major Motion Picture from Twentieth Century Fox

The Tiger Rising

The Tiger Rising is a sad story. The main character in this story, Rob Horton, is **withdrawn** and afraid. Rob moves to a new town with his father after his mother dies. They live in a motel, where Rob's father works as caretaker. Some students at school bully Rob. He develops a rash in reaction to the bullying.

One day, Rob finds a fearsome, caged tiger in the woods. Then, Rob meets Sistine Bailey, a girl who is almost as frightening as the tiger. Rob and the **defiant** Sistine join together to free the tiger.

The Tiger Rising is a story about loneliness and the importance of friends. It also shows the happiness that comes when parents and children understand one another.

AWARDS
The Tiger Rising
2002 National Book Award

2001 Parents' Choice Award

2002 Oppenheim Toy Portfolio Award

The Tale of Despereaux

In *The Tale of Despereaux*, Kate DiCamillo plays the role of the storyteller. As storyteller, she encourages readers to continue reading. Kate also teaches the use of **context** clues in understanding words and explains important points in the story.

The Tale of Despereaux contains four different stories. The first story is about Despereaux Tilling. He is a tiny mouse with very large ears. Despereaux is in love with music, stories, and a princess named Pea. The second story tells of a rat named Roscuro. Roscuro has a deep love for light and soup. The third story is about Miggery Sow. She is a poor serving girl who believes she can become a princess. The final story links Despereaux, Roscuro, Miggery Sow, and Princess Pea.

The Tale of Despereaux contains many serious **themes**. One sad theme is that families are not always loyal and loving. Another theme is that hope, love, and forgiveness can change people's hearts and make a difference in the world.

This story is serious but not **grim**. *The Tale of Despereaux* is lighthearted in some places. Kate tells the story in an enjoyable way. Some characters speak in amusing ways, but the storyteller is always formal and elegant.

KATE DiCAMILLO
author of *Because of Winn-Dixie*

The Tale of Despereaux

illustrated by *Timothy Basil Ering*

Because of Winn-Dixie Screenplay

Kate accepted a new challenge when her book, *Because of Winn-Dixie* became a movie. Producer/screenwriter Joan Singleton purchased the book for her daughter. After her daughter read the book, she insisted that Joan read it as well. Joan read the book and thought it would make a wonderful movie. She wrote the first script.

Scriptwriting is very different from novel writing. Kate was asked to help rewrite the script to make sure that the feelings expressed in the book and the movie were the same. Kate is delighted with the movie. She says, "It's funny and it's beautiful."

AnnaSophia Robb plays India Opal Buloni in the movie, *Because of Winn-Dixie*. AnnaSophia said she enjoyed acting as India Opal and playing with the dog.

Creative Writing Tips

K ate DiCamillo's published books prove that she knows how to make characters seem real, how to describe a scene, and how to handle words. Kate says that anyone who wants to write should read, write, look, listen, and know their audience.

> "We (writers) get our ideas from listening and looking and eavesdropping and imagining. Stories are everywhere. All you have to do is pay attention."
> Kate DiCamillo

Read

Kate read many books as a child. Through her English degree, she has training in reading. She thanks other writers for being **mentors**. She is grateful to the writers of the many good books that she has read.

Write

Kate spent 14 years dreaming about writing before she actually began to write. When she began writing, she followed a schedule. This forced her to write at the same time every day.

Look

Writers make their stories seem real by looking at their surroundings and using realistic details in their stories. While driving one day, Kate saw a tree covered in bottles. That detail is in *Because of Winn-Dixie*. Gloria Dump's jacaranda tree is covered in bottles.

Kate believes writers should use their imaginations. Writers can combine details from their imaginations with real events.

Listen

When Kate began writing *Because of Winn-Dixie*, she could hear a little girl with a southern accent in her mind. If writers listen, they will hear the words and accents that people use when they speak. When writers begin their stories, their characters sound like real people.

Audience

Writers must always remember who their readers will be. Kate worked with children in several jobs. She knows her audience. When Luke Bailey, a friend's son, asked her to write a story about an unlucky hero with big ears, Kate listened. She thought about his request and wrote about a heroic mouse in *The Tale of Despereaux*.

Inspired to Write

According to Kate, there is no right or wrong way to tell a story. This is what makes writing both wonderful and terrifying. Kate says writers must try to find their own way to tell stories.

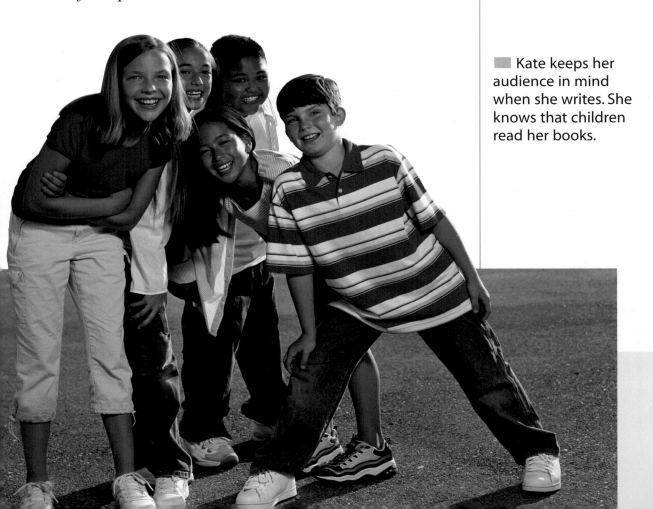

Kate keeps her audience in mind when she writes. She knows that children read her books.

Writing a Biography Review

A biography is an account of an individual's life that is written by another person. Some people's lives are very interesting. In school, you may be asked to write a biography review. The first thing to do when writing a biography review is to decide whom you would like to learn about. Your school library or community library will have a large selection of biographies from which to choose.

Are you interested in an author, a sports figure, an inventor, a movie star, or a president? Finding the right book is your first task. Whether you choose to write your review on a biography of Kate DiCamillo or another person, the task will be similar.

Begin your review by writing the title of the book, the author, and the person featured in the book. Then, start writing about the main events in the person's life. Include such things as where the person grew up and what his or her childhood was like. You will want to add details about the person's adult life, such as whether he or she married or had children. Next, write about what you think makes this person special. What kinds of experiences influenced this individual? For instance, did he or she grow up in unusual circumstances? Was the person determined to accomplish a goal? Include any details that surprised you. A concept web is a useful research tool. Use the concept web on the right to begin researching your biography review.

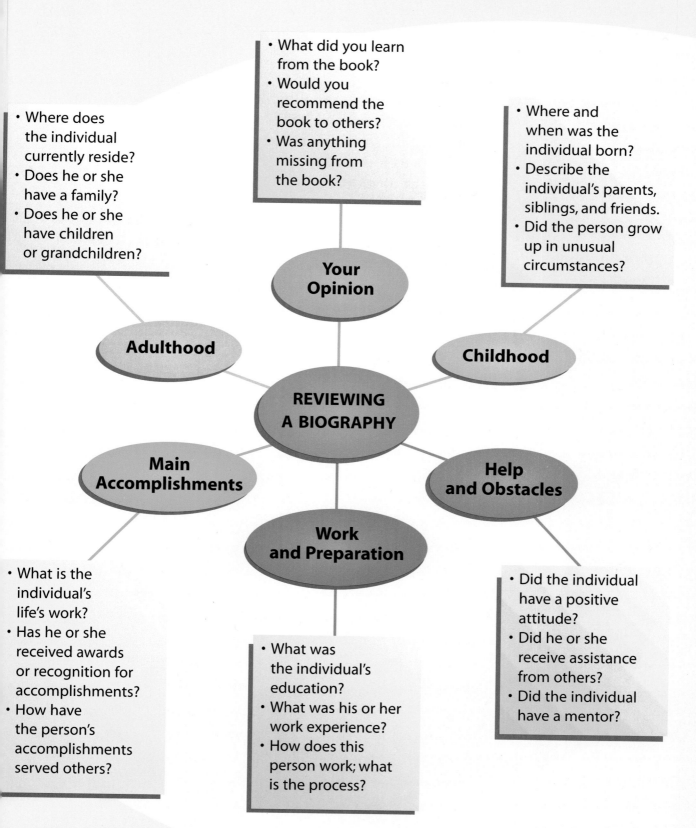

- Where does the individual currently reside?
- Does he or she have a family?
- Does he or she have children or grandchildren?

- What did you learn from the book?
- Would you recommend the book to others?
- Was anything missing from the book?

- Where and when was the individual born?
- Describe the individual's parents, siblings, and friends.
- Did the person grow up in unusual circumstances?

Your Opinion

Adulthood

Childhood

REVIEWING A BIOGRAPHY

Main Accomplishments

Help and Obstacles

Work and Preparation

- What is the individual's life's work?
- Has he or she received awards or recognition for accomplishments?
- How have the person's accomplishments served others?

- What was the individual's education?
- What was his or her work experience?
- How does this person work; what is the process?

- Did the individual have a positive attitude?
- Did he or she receive assistance from others?
- Did the individual have a mentor?

Fan Information

Kate enjoys meeting her fans. She describes herself as "short and loud." Kate is about 5 feet (1.5 meters) tall, so she is not much taller than many of her fans. Kate loves to visit schools. She likes to speak to school groups and answer fans' questions.

Children have written Kate letters saying that *Because of Winn-Dixie* has made them like reading. Kate says, "Hands down, the biggest thrill is to get a letter from a kid saying, 'I loved your book. Will you write me another one?'"

Since Kate has won many important awards, she finds herself very busy. Kate is booked into festivals, schools and interviews well into the future.

In 2004, Kate received the Newbery Medal for *The Tale of Despereaux*. Cynthia Richey, president of the Association for Library Service to Children, presented the award.

Kate's third novel, *The Tale of Despereaux*, is also being made into a movie. As well, she is working on a collection of short stories for adults. Her fans eagerly await her next novel, *The Miraculous Journey of Edward Tulane*.

A mouse, a princess, some soup, and a spool of thread ...

Rob, a caged tiger in the Florida woods, and a girl named Sistine ...

India Opal Buloni, a dog discovered at Winn-Dixie, and the people who live in Naomi ...

these are the books that Kate has already written.

She's very busy writing more.

Because of Winn-Dixie, the MOVIE!
Walden Media invites reading teachers, English Language Arts teachers, and librarian/media specialists to register to win a FREE PASS for two to attend an advance screening of *Because of Winn-Dixie* in early February.

The movie version of *Because of Winn-Dixie* will be in movie theaters beginning February 18th. If you'd like to take a peek at the movie, visit the Walden Media website.

WEB LINKS

Kate DiCamillo's Home Page

www.katedicamillo.com

To learn about Kate's life and her books, visit this Web site.

An Interview with Kate

www.kidsreads.com/authors/au-dicamillo-kate.asp

Visit this Web site to read a brief biography of Kate. You can also read an interview with her. She talks about how she came to be a writer and the success of her first book.

Quiz

Q: When and where was Kate DiCamillo born?

A: March 25, 1964, in Philadelphia, Pennsylvania.

1

Q: Where did Kate move when she was 5 years old?

A: Kate moved to Clermont, Florida.

2

Q: From which university did Kate receive an English degree?

A: The University of Florida in Gainesville

3

Q: Where was Kate working when she began to read children's books as an adult?

A: A book warehouse

Q: What is the name of Kate's first book?

A: *Because of Winn-Dixie*

Q: For which book did Kate win the Newbery Medal?

A: *The Tale of Despereaux*

Q: Who asked Kate to write about a hero with big ears?

A: Luke Bailey, a friend's son

Q: Where does Kate live now?

A: Minneapolis, Minnesota

Q: How many children does Kate have?

A: Kate does not have any children.

Q: Who is the main character in *Because of Winn-Dixie*?

A: India Opal Buloni

Writing Terms

This glossary will introduce you to some of the main terms in the field of writing. Understanding these common writing terms will allow you to discuss your ideas about books and writing with others.

action: the moving events of a work of fiction

antagonist: the person in the story who opposes the main character

autobiography: a history of a person's life written by that person

biography: a written account of another person's life

character: a person in a story, poem, or play

climax: the most exciting moment or turning point in a story

episode: a short piece of action, or scene, in a story

fiction: stories about characters and events that are not real

foreshadow: hinting at something that is going to happen later in the book

imagery: a written description of a thing or idea that brings an image to mind

narrator: the speaker of the story who relates the events

nonfiction: writing that deals with real people and events

novel: published writing of considerable length that portrays characters within a story

plot: the order of events in a work of fiction

protagonist: the leading character of a story; often a likable character

resolution: the end of the story, when the conflict is settled

scene: a single episode in a story

setting: the place and time in which a work of fiction occurs

theme: an idea that runs throughout a work of fiction

Glossary

complicated: difficult to understand

context: words before and after a word or phrase that give clues to meaning

critique: a critical review on a subject or literary work

cultural: related to the customs, traditions, and values of a nation or people

defiant: aggressively opposed to

draft: a rough copy of something written

epiphany: a sudden perception or realization

grant: money awarded for a specific reason or cause

grim: harsh or unpleasant

majestic: grand or noble

manuscripts: drafts of stories before they are published

marginally: slightly

mentors: experienced advisors and supporters

persevere: keep on trying

pines: longs for; really wants

recurring: taking place over and over again

themes: ideas that run throughout works of fiction

torment: suffering; agony

whittled: carved a piece of wood

withdrawn: removed or reserved

Index

Photo Credits

Cover: Brett Patterson
AP/Wide World Photo: page 26; Kristen Bartlett/University of Florida: page 9; courtesy of Candlewick Press: pages 18, 19, 20; Getty Images: page 10 (Tony Ranze/AFP), 11 (Brand X Pictures), 13 (Altrendo), 22 (Brand X Pictures), 23 (PhotoDisc Red); Lake County Historical Society: pages 7, 8; Brett Patterson: pages 1, 3, 4, 12, 16; Photofest: pages 17, 21; Joe Rossi/Pioneer Press: page 28.